P9-CSS-493

This workbook is designed to help young children develop the skills for both oral and written communication. Skills in basic phonics, such as consonant and vowel sounds are reinforced, while more involved phonetic skills, such as digraphs, diphthongs, and blends are introduced. Sentence structure and word usage skills, such as compound words, antonyms, homonyms, synonyms, and parts of speech are included. Present and past tense, as well as exercises in reading and writing sentences for greater meaning, are introduced. This workbook is one in a series of high interest workbooks designed to help children master the English language.

Table of Contents

Continued next page

Table of Contents (Continued)

Glossary

Antonyms. Words that are opposites.

Adjectives. Words that describe nouns. Example: fuzzy, chewy, hard, soft.

Articles. Small words that help us better understand nouns. Example: "a" or "an."

Beginning Consonants. Sounds that come at the beginning of words that are not vowel sounds. (Vowels are the letters a, e, i, o, u and sometimes y.)

Blends. When two sounds are put together, but we hear both sounds. Example: "bl" in blend.

Command. A sentence that tells someone to do something. Example: Fix it.

Compound Words. When two words are put together to make one word. Example: house + boat = houseboat.

Contractions. A short way to write two words together, such as isn't for is not.

Digraphs. When two sounds are put together, but we hear only one sound. Example: "ea" in sweater or "ch" in cheese.

Diphthongs. When two sounds are put together to make two new sounds. Example: "oi" in oil.

Homonyms. Words that sound the same but are spelled differently and mean different things. Example: blue and blew.

Nouns. Words that tell the names of people, places or things.

Pronouns. Words that can be used instead of nouns. Example: he, she, it, they.

Sentence. A group of words that tells a whole idea or asks a question.

Synonyms. Words that mean the same.

Verbs. The action word in a sentence.

Name: _____

Consonants: B,C,D,F,G,H,J

Directions: Look at the pictures with the arrows next to them. Write the letter that makes the beginning sound for each word on the lines below.

1	2	3	4	5	6	7
__	__	__	__	__	__	__

Consonants K, L, M, N, P, Q, R

Directions: Write the letter that makes the beginning sound for each picture.

_____ _____ _____ _____

_____ _____ _____ _____

_____ _____ _____ _____

_____ _____ _____ _____

Name: _____

Consonants: S, T, V, W, X, Y, Z

Directions: Write the letter that makes the beginning sound under each picture.

Name: _____

Short Vowels

Vowels can make "short" or "long" sounds. The short "a" sounds like the "a" in cat. The short "e" is like the "e" in leg. The short "i" sounds like the "i" in pig. The short "o" sounds like the "o" in box. The short "u" sounds like the "u" in cup.

Directions: Look at each picture. Write the missing short vowel letter.

p _____ p

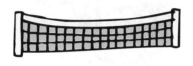

n _____ t

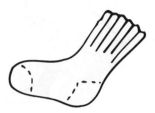

s _____ ck

_____ x

l _____ ps

h _____ t

f _____ x

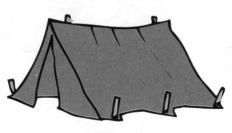

t _____ nt

p _____ n

Name: _____

Short Vowels

Directions: 1) Say the name of the pictures at the top of the page. 2) Listen for the short vowel sounds. 3) Read the sentences below. 4) Circle the words that have the same short vowel sound as the letter at the beginning of the sentence.

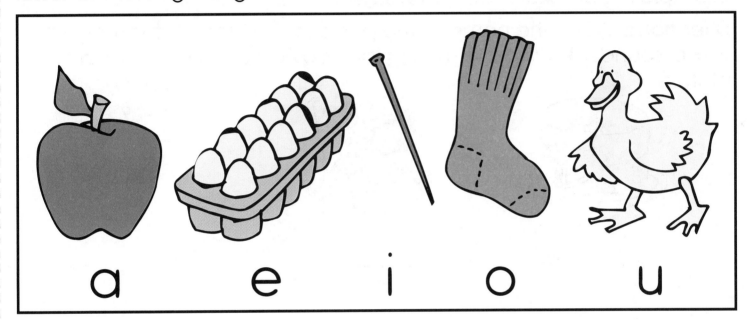

a   e   i   o   u

Ee	Ed and Ted went to bed.
Aa	Mac and Sam have a lamb.
Uu	It is fun to play in the sun.
Oo	She lost her sock on the rock.
Ii	The pig can fit in the bin.

Name: _____

Long Vowels

Long Vowel sounds have the same sound as their names (like the "e" in bee). When a "Super e" appears at the end of a word, you can't hear it, but it makes the other vowel have a long sound.

Examples: rope, skate, bee, pie, suit.

Directions: 1) Say the name of the pictures. 2) Listen for the long vowel sounds. 3) Write the missing long vowel sound under each picture.

c _____ ke

h _____ ke

n _____ se

b _____ et

t _____ be

p _____ a

r _____ ke

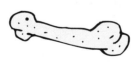

b _____ ne

k _____ te

Name: _____

Long Vowels

Directions: Look in the word bank to find out what Jane and Pete are taking on their space trip. Circle the long vowel words in the word puzzle.

| skate | suit | rope | seeds | tree | cake | boat |
| pie | eagle | ape | beans | soap | fruit | |

B E D S K A T E O T U B N E T R O P E

C A K E C O Z R T R E E V B N B O A T

Y I P T P I E Z I N E A G L E Q A P E

B E A N S T R B S O A P B V F R U I T

W E R S U I T U I P S E E D S A Q P R

Name: _____

Review

Directions: Write the word from the word bank under the picture. Circle the beginning consonant. Color the objects red if the vowel sound is short. Color the objects blue if the vowel sound is long.

goat	fan	cage	dog	hat	rope
jar	pie	bed	tube	vase	pot

_____ _____ _____ _____

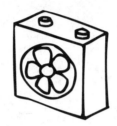

_____ _____ _____ _____

_____ _____ _____ _____

Digraphs: au, aw, oo

(When two letters are put together to make one new sound.)

Directions: 1) Look at the first picture in each row. 2) Say the name.
3) Circle the objects that have the same sound.

faucet

saw

boots

cook

Name: _____

Digraphs: au, aw, oo

Directions: Say the words in the word bank. Find them in the word puzzle and circle them.

feather	awning	pool	laundry
head	claw	sweater	book

p o t v b r p o o l b a h n h e a d

a w n i n g l e r e s w e a t e r q

y u i c l a w b o r d b o o k r t y

f e a t h e r c a y u l a u n d r y

10

Digraphs: wh, sh, ch, th

Directions: 1) Look at the first picture in each row. 2) Say the name. 3) Circle the objects that have the same sound.

whistle

shoe

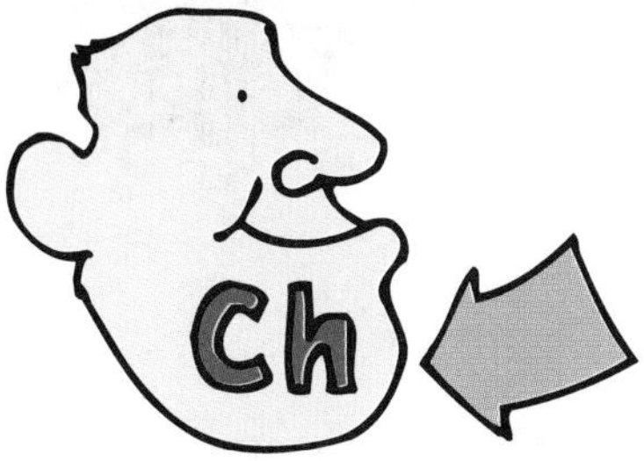

chin

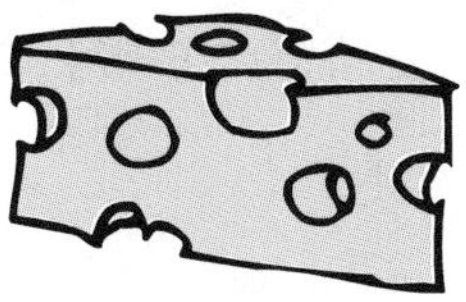

thumb

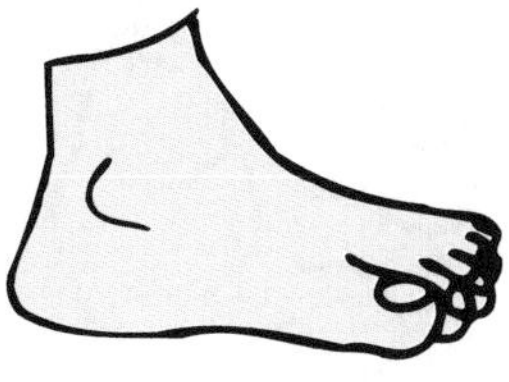

Name: _____

Digraphs: sh, ch, wh, th

Directions: Look at the pictures and say the word. Write the first two letters of the word on the space below each picture.

_____

_____

_____

_____

_____

_____

_____

_____

_____

Name: _____

Dipthongs: oi, oy, ou, ow

(Putting two letters together to make two new sounds.)

Directions: 1) Look at the first picture in each row. 2) Say the name.
3) Circle the objects that have the same sound.

Name: _____

Blends: fl, br, sk, sn

(When two sounds are put together, but we hear both sounds.)

Directions: Look at the pictures and say their names. Write the letters for the first two sounds in each word.

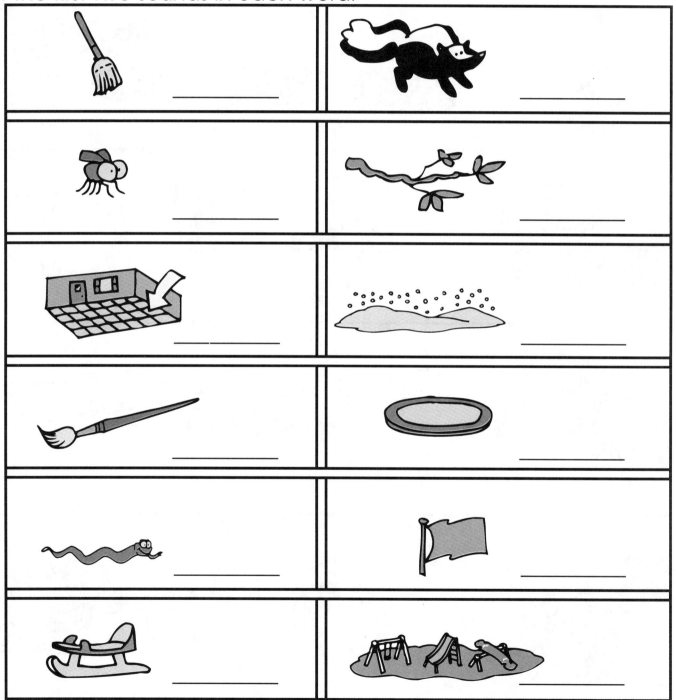

14

Name: _____

Blends: bl, sl, cr, cl

Directions: Look at the pictures and say their names. Write the letters for the first two sounds you hear in each word.

_____ own

_____ anket

_____ ayon

_____ ock

_____ ide

_____ oud

_____ ed

_____ ab

_____ ocodile

Name: _____

Review

Directions: Write the correct 2-letter blends in the first box of pictures. Write the 2-letter diphthongs in the second box.

| branch | cloud | skunk | cheese | crayon | snake |
| blanket | thorn | whistle | sheep | playground | |

_____   _____   _____   _____   _____

_____   _____   _____   _____   _____

| owl | boil | moon | paw | faucet | boy | couch | book |

_____   _____   _____   _____

_____   _____   _____   _____

Name: _____

y As a Vowel That Sounds Like e

Directions: Read the silly story. Choose the words from the word bank to fill in the blanks.

Larry	Mary
money	funny
honey	bunny

_____ and _____ are friends.   Larry is

selling _____ .   Mary needs _____ to

buy the honey.   "I want to feed it to my _____ ," said

Mary.   Larry laughed and said, "That is _____ ."

Everyone knows that bunnies do not eat honey.

Name: _____

y As a Vowel That Sounds Like i

Directions: Read the story. Choose the words from the word bank to fill in the blanks.

| try | my | Why | cry | shy | fly |

Sam is very _____ . Ann asks, "Would you like to

_____ my kite?" Sam starts to _____ .

Ann asks, "_____ are you crying?" Sam says, " I am

afraid to _____ ."

"Oh_____ ! You are

a good kite flyer." cries Ann.

R-Controlled Words

R-Controlled words are words in which the "r" that immediately follows the vowel changes the sound of the vowel. Example: bird, star, burn.

Directions: Write the correct word in the sentences below.

horse	purple
jar	bird
dirt	turtle

1. Jelly comes in one of these.

_____

2. This creature has feathers and can fly.

_____

3. This animal lives in a shell.

_____

4. This animal can pull wagons.

_____

5. If you mix water with this, you will have mud.

_____

6. This color starts with the letter 'p'.

_____

Name: _____

Compound Words

Compound words are two words that are put together to make one.

Directions: Read the sentences. Fill in the blank with a compound word from the word bank.

| raincoat | bedroom | lunchbox | hallway | sandbox |

1. A box with sand is a

_____

_____

2. The way through a hall is a

_____

_____

3. A box for lunch is a

_____

_____

4. A coat for the rain is a

_____

_____

5. A room with a bed is a

_____

_____

Name: _____

Antonyms

Directions: Read the words next to the pictures. Draw a line to the word that means the opposite.

dark

empty

hairy

dry

closed

happy

dirty

bald

sad

clean

full

light

wet

open

21

Name: _____

Synonyms

Directions: Read the story and fill in the blanks with the word that has the same meaning.

funny	unhappy
windy	little

A New Balloon

It was a breezy day. The wind blew the small child's balloon away. The child was sad. A silly clown gave him a new balloon.

1. It was a _____ day.

2. The wind blew the _____ child's balloon away.

3. The child was _____ .

4. A _____ clown gave him a new balloon.

Name: _____

Homonyms

Directions: Write the word from the word bank that has the same sound but a different meaning next to each picture.

| so | see | blew | pear |

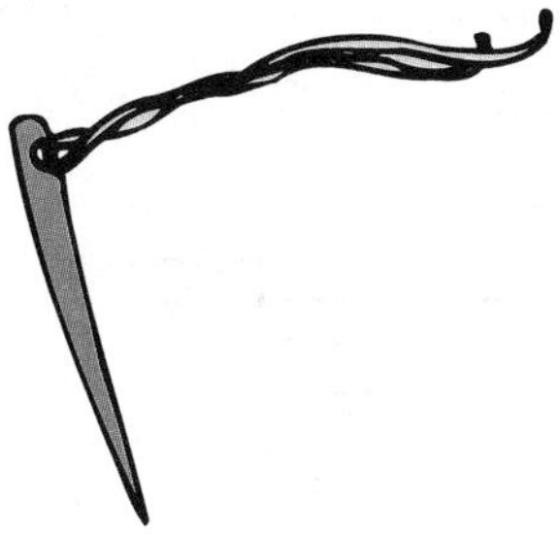

sew   _____

pair   _____

sea   _____

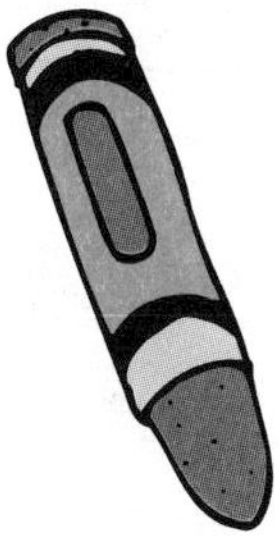

blue   _____

Name: _____

Review

Directions: Fill in each blank with a word from the word bank.

fawn	toys	dry	hot	sweater
boil	burn	cherry	star	

1. Be careful not to _____ your hand.

2. I like to eat _____ pie.

3. The dog was wet but now it is _____ .

4. The baby likes to play with _____ .

5. A baby deer is called a _____ .

6. The water in the pot will _____ .

7. The opposite of cold is _____ .

8. Wear a _____ on a cold day.

9. A _____ shines in the sky at night.

Name: _____

Nouns

The name of a person, place, or thing is a noun.

Directions: Read the story and circle all the nouns. Then, write the nouns next to the pictures below.

Our family likes to go

to the park.

We play on the swings.

We eat cake.

We drink lemonade.

We throw the ball to

our dog.

Then, we go home.

_____
_____
_____
_____
_____
_____
_____
_____
_____
_____
_____
_____
_____
_____
_____
_____
_____
_____
_____
_____
_____

Plural Nouns

Plural nouns name more than one person, place, or thing.

Directions: Read the words in the word bank. Write the words in the correct column.

| hats | spoons | girl | glass | cows | book | kittens | horse | cake |

Name: _____

Pronouns

Pronouns are words that can be used instead of nouns. "She," "he," "it" and "they" are pronouns.

Directions: Read the sentence. Then write the sentence again, using She, He, It or They in the blank.

1. Dan likes funny jokes. _____ likes funny jokes.

2. Peg and Sam went to the zoo. _____ went to the zoo.

3. My dog likes to dig in the yard. _____ likes to dig in the yard.

4. Sara is a very good dancer. _____ is a very good dancer.

5. Fred and Ted are twins. _____ are twins.

Articles

Articles are small words that help us to better understand nouns. "A" and "an" are articles. We use "an" before a word that begins with a vowel. We use "a" before a word that begins with a consonant.

Example: We looked in **a** nest. It had **an** eagle in it.

Directions: Read the sentences. Write an "a" or an "an" in the blank.

1. I found _____ book.

2. It had a story about _____ ant in it.

3. In the story, _____ lion gave three wishes to _____ ant.

4. The ant's first wish was to ride _____ elephant.

5. The second wish was to ride _____ alligator.

6. The last wish was _____ wish for three more wishes.

Name: _____

Verbs

A verb is the action word in a sentence; the word that tells what something does or that something exists.

Examples: "run," "sleep," "jump" are verbs.

Directions: Circle the verbs in the sentences below.

1. We play baseball everyday.

2. Susan pitches the ball very well.

3. Mike swings the bat harder than anyone.

4. Chris can slide into home base.

5. Laura can hit a home run.

Name: _____

Verbs

We use verbs to tell when something happens. Sometimes we add an "ed" to verbs that tell us if something has already happened.

Example: Today, we play. Yesterday, we played.

Directions: Write the correct verb in the blank.

1. Today, I will _____ my dog, Fritz.

                     wash, washed

2. Last week, Fritz _____ when we said, "Bath time, Fritz."

                     cry, cried

3. My sister likes to _____ wash Fritz.

                     help, helped

4. One time she _____ Fritz by herself.

                     clean, cleaned

5. Fritz will _____ a lot better after his bath.

                     look, looked

ANSWER KEY

*This Answer Key has been designed so that
it may be easily removed if you so desire.*

MASTER ENGLISH
2

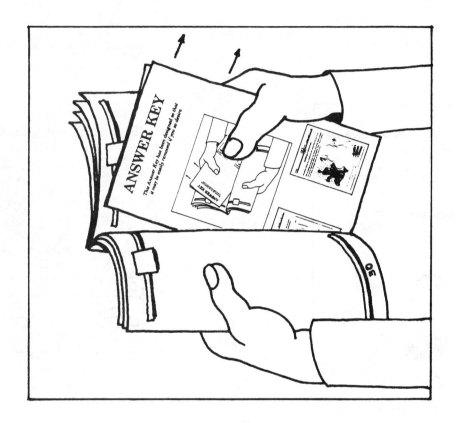

Consonants: B,C,D,F,G,H,J

Directions: Look at the pictures with the arrows next to them. Write the letter that makes the beginning sound for each word on the lines below.

1	2	3	4	5	6	7
f	c	b	g	j	h	d

Consonants K, L, M, N, P, Q, R

Directions: Write the letter that makes the beginning sound for each picture.

r q p n

m l k r

q p n m

l k r p

Consonants: S, T, V, W, X, Y, Z

Directions: Write the letter that makes the beginning sound under each picture.

s   z   x

v   y

w   t

Long Vowels

Long Vowel sounds have the same sound as their names (like the "e" in bee). When a "Super e" appears at the end of a word, you can't hear it, but it makes the other vowel have a long sound.

Examples: rope, skate, bee, pie, suit.

Directions: 1) Say the name of the pictures. 2) Listen for the long vowel sounds. 3) Write the missing long vowel sound under each picture.

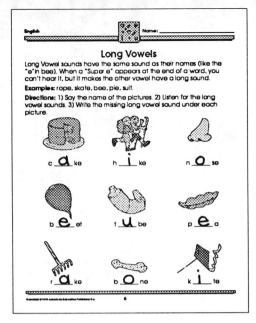

c a ke   h i ke   n o se

b e et   t u be   p e a

r a ke   b o ne   k i te

Short Vowels

Vowels can make "short" or "long" sounds. The short "a" sounds like the "a" in cat. The short "e" is like the "e" in leg. The short "i" sounds like the "i" in pig. The short "o" sounds like the "o" in box. The short "u" sounds like the "u" in cup.

Directions: Look at each picture. Write the missing short vowel letter.

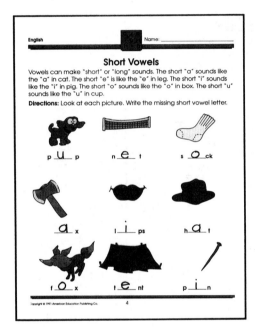

p u p   n e t   s o ck

a x   l i ps   h a t

f o x   t e nt   p i n

Long Vowels

Directions: Look in the word bank to find out what Jane and Pete are taking on their space trip. Circle the long vowel words in the word puzzle.

skate	suit	rope	seeds	tree	cake	boat
pie	eagle	ape	beans	soap	fruit	

```
B E D (S K A T E) O T U B N E T (R O P E)
(C A K E) C O Z R (T R E E) V B N (B O A T)
Y 1 P T (P I E) Z 1 N (E A G L E) Q (A P E)
(B E A N S) T R B (S O A P) B V (F R U I T)
W E R (S U I T) U 1 P (S E E D S) A Q P R
```

Short Vowels

Directions: 1) Say the name of the pictures at the top of the page. 2) Listen for the short vowel sounds. 3) Read the sentences below. 4) Circle the words that have the same short vowel sound as the letter at the beginning of the sentence.

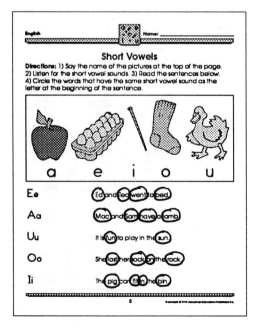

a   e   i   o   u

Ee   (Ed) and (Ted) (went) to (bed).

Aa   (Mac) and (Sam) (have) a (lamb).

Uu   It is (fun) to play in the (sun).

Oo   She (lost) her (sock) on the (rock).

Ii   The (pig) can (fish) in the (bin).

Review

Directions: Write the word from the word bank under the picture. Circle the beginning consonant. Color the objects red if the vowel sound is short. Color the objects blue if the vowel sound is short.

lamb	fan	cage	dog	hat	rope
jar	pie	bed	tube	vase	pot

bed   fan   cage   tube

jar   goat   hat   pot

vase   pie   dog   rope

Digraphs: au, aw, oo
(When two letters are put together to make one new sound.)
Directions: 1) Look at the first picture in each row. 2) Say the name. 3) Circle the objects that have the same sound.

faucet

saw

boots

cook

9

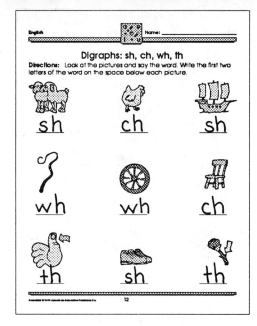

Digraphs: sh, ch, wh, th
Directions: Look at the pictures and say the word. Write the first two letters of the word on the space below each picture.

sh   ch   sh

wh   wh   ch

th   sh   th

12

Digraphs: au, aw, oo
Directions: Say the words in the word bank. Find them in the word puzzle and circle them.

oo   oo   au   ea

| feather | awning | pool | laundry |
| head | claw | sweater | book |

p o t v b r p o o l b a h n h e a d
a w n i n g l e r e s w e a t e r q
y u i c l a w b o r d b o o k r t y
f e a t h e r c a y u l a u n d r y

10

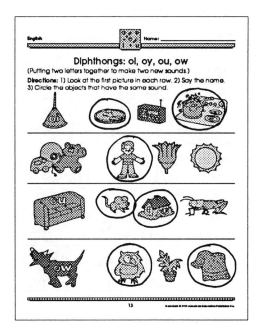

Diphthongs: oi, oy, ou, ow
(Putting two letters together to make two new sounds.)
Directions: 1) Look at the first picture in each row. 2) Say the name. 3) Circle the objects that have the same sound.

13

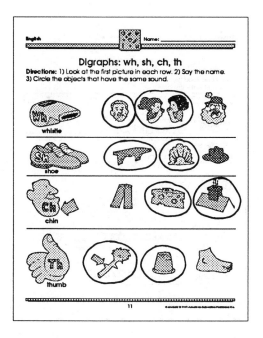

Digraphs: wh, sh, ch, th
Directions: 1) Look at the first picture in each row. 2) Say the name. 3) Circle the objects that have the same sound.

wh
whistle

sh
shoe

ch
chin

th
thumb

11

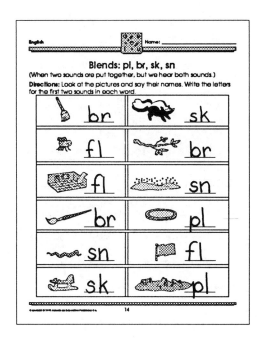

Blends: pl, br, sk, sn
(When two sounds are put together, but we hear both sounds.)
Directions: Look at the pictures and say their names. Write the letters for the first two sounds in each word.

br	sk
fl	br
fl	sn
br	pl
sn	fl
sk	pl

14

Blends: bl, sl, cr, cl

Directions: Look at the pictures and say their names. Write the letters for the first two sounds you hear in each word.

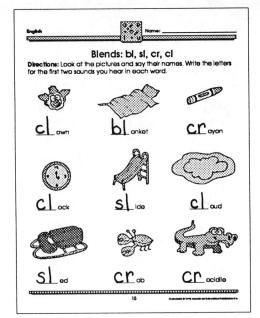

cl own   bl anket   cr ayon

cl ock   sl ide   cl oud

sl ed   cr ab   cr ocodile

---

y As a Vowel That Sounds Like i

Directions: Read the story. Choose the words from the word bank to fill in the blanks.

try	my	Why	cry	shy	fly

Sam is very **shy** . Ann asks, "Would you like to

fly my kite?" Sam starts to **cry**

Ann asks, "**Why** are you crying?" Sam says, " I am

afraid to **try** .

"Oh **my** ! You are

a good kite flyer." cries Ann.

Review

Directions: Write the correct 2-letter blends in the first box of pictures. Write the 2-letter diphthongs in the second box.

branch	cloud	skunk	cheese	crayon	snake
blanket	thorn	whistle	sheep	playground	

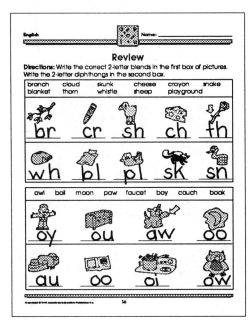

br cr sh ch th

wh bl pl sk sn

owl	boil	moon	paw	faucet	boy	couch	book

oy ou aw oo

au oo oi ow

R-Controlled Words

R-Controlled words are words in which the "r" that immediately follows the vowel changes the sound of the vowel. Example: bird, star, burn.

Directions: Write the correct word in the sentences below.

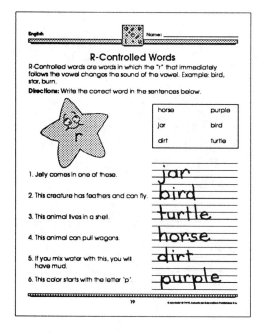

horse	purple
jar	bird
dirt	turtle

1. Jelly comes in one of these. **jar**

2. This creature has feathers and can fly. **bird**

3. This animal lives in a shell. **turtle**

4. This animal can pull wagons. **horse**

5. If you mix water with this, you will have mud. **dirt**

6. This color starts with the letter 'p'. **purple**

---

y As a Vowel That Sounds Like e

Directions: Read the silly story. Choose the words from the word bank to fill in the blanks.

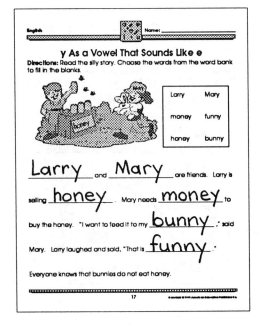

Larry	Mary
money	funny
honey	bunny

Larry and **Mary** are friends. Larry is

selling **honey** . Mary needs **money** to

buy the honey. "I want to feed it to my **bunny** ," said

Mary. Larry laughed and said, "That is **funny** ."

Everyone knows that bunnies do not eat honey.

Compound Words

Compound words are two words that are put together to make one.

Directions: Read the sentences. Fill in the blank with a compound word from the word bank.

raincoat	bedroom	lunchbox	hallway	sandbox

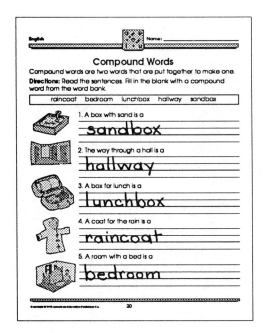

1. A box with sand is a **sandbox**

2. The way through a hall is a **hallway**

3. A box for lunch is a **lunchbox**

4. A coat for the rain is a **raincoat**

5. A room with a bed is a **bedroom**

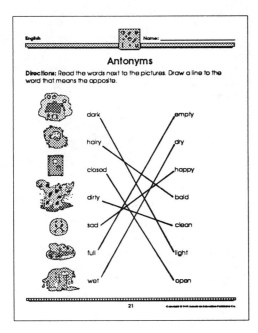

Antonyms

Directions: Read the words next to the pictures. Draw a line to the word that means the opposite.

dark — empty
hairy — dry
closed — happy
dirty — bald
sad — clean
full — light
wet — open

21

Synonyms

Directions: Read the story and fill in the blanks with the word that has the same meaning.

| funny | unhappy |
| windy | little |

A New Balloon

It was a breezy day. The wind blew the small child's balloon away. The child was sad. A silly clown gave him a new balloon.

1. It was a **windy** day.

2. The wind blew the **little** child's balloon away.

3. The child was **unhappy**.

4. A **funny** clown gave him a new balloon.

22

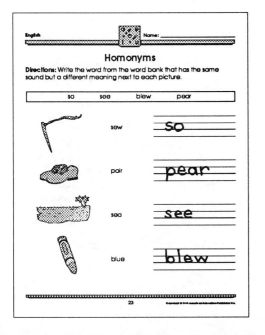

Homonyms

Directions: Write the word from the word bank that has the same sound but a different meaning next to each picture.

| so | see | blew | pear |

sew — **so**

pair — **pear**

sea — **see**

blue — **blew**

23

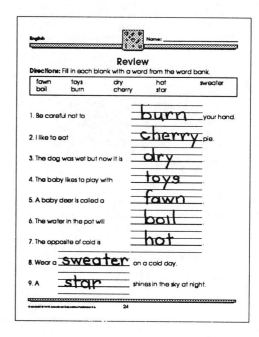

Review

Directions: Fill in each blank with a word from the word bank.

| fawn | toys | dry | hot | sweater |
| boil | burn | cherry | star | |

1. Be careful not to **burn** your hand.

2. I like to eat **cherry** pie.

3. The dog was wet but now it is **dry**

4. The baby likes to play with **toys**

5. A baby deer is called a **fawn**

6. The water in the pot will **boil**

7. The opposite of cold is **hot**

8. Wear a **sweater** on a cold day.

9. A **star** shines in the sky at night.

24

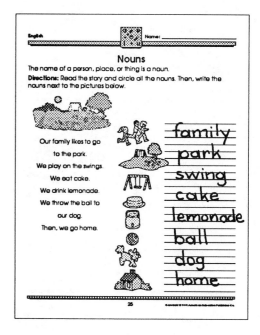

Nouns

The name of a person, place, or thing is a noun.

Directions: Read the story and circle all the nouns. Then, write the nouns next to the pictures below.

Our family likes to go to the park. We play on the swings. We eat cake. We drink lemonade. We throw the ball to our dog. Then, we go home.

family
park
swing
cake
lemonade
ball
dog
home

25

Plural Nouns

Plural nouns name more than one person, place, or thing.

Directions: Read the words in the word bank. Write the words in the correct column.

| hats spoons girl glass cows book kittens horse cake |

one / more than one

girl — **hats**
glass — **spoons**
book — **cows**
horse — **kittens**
cake

26

Pronouns

Pronouns are words that can be used instead of nouns. "She," "he," "it" and "they" are pronouns.

Directions: Read the sentence. Then write the sentence again, using She, He, It or They in the blank.

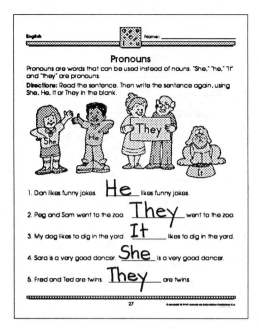

1. Dan likes funny jokes. **He** likes funny jokes.

2. Peg and Sam went to the zoo. **They** went to the zoo.

3. My dog likes to dig in the yard. **It** likes to dig in the yard.

4. Sara is a very good dancer. **She** is a very good dancer.

5. Fred and Ted are twins. **They** are twins.

27

Verbs

We use verbs to tell when something happens. Sometimes we add an "ed" to verbs that tell us if something has already happened.

Example: Today, we play. Yesterday, we played.

Directions: Write the correct verb in the blank.

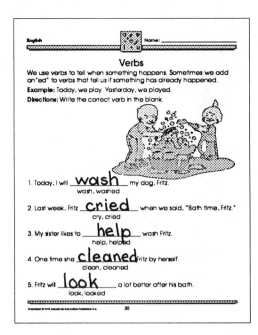

1. Today, I will **wash** my dog, Fritz.
   wash, washed

2. Last week, Fritz **cried** when we said, "Bath time, Fritz."
   cry, cried

3. My sister likes to **help** wash Fritz.
   help, helped

4. One time she **cleaned** Fritz by herself.
   clean, cleaned

5. Fritz will **look** a lot better after his bath.
   look, looked

30

Articles

Articles are small words that help us to better understand nouns. "A" and "an" are articles. We use "an" before a word that begins with a vowel. We use "a" before a word that begins with a consonant.

Example: We looked in **a** nest. It had **an** eagle in it.

Directions: Read the sentences. Write an "a" or an "an" in the blank.

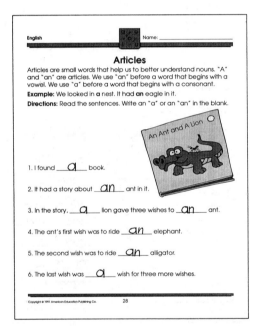

1. I found **a** book.

2. It had a story about **an** ant in it.

3. In the story, **a** lion gave three wishes to **an** ant.

4. The ant's first wish was to ride **an** elephant.

5. The second wish was to ride **an** alligator.

6. The last wish was **a** wish for three more wishes.

Copyright © 1991 American Education Publishing Co.   28

Verbs

Directions: Write each verb in the correct column.

| rake | talked | look | hopped | skip |
| cooked | fished | call | clean | sewed |

Yesterday	Today
talked	rake
hopped	look
cooked	skip
fished	call
sewed	clean

31

Verbs

A verb is the action word in a sentence; the word that tells what something does or that something exists.

Example: "run," "sleep," "jump" are verbs.

Directions: Circle the verbs in the sentences below.

1. We **play** baseball everyday.

2. Susan **pitches** the ball very well.

3. Mike **swings** the bat harder than anyone.

4. Chris can **slide** into home base.

5. Laura can **hit** a home run.

29

Review

Directions: Read the sentences. Draw a blue circle around the nouns. Draw a red line under the articles, "a" and "an". Draw a green square around the pronouns, she, he, it, or they. Draw an orange triangle around the verbs.

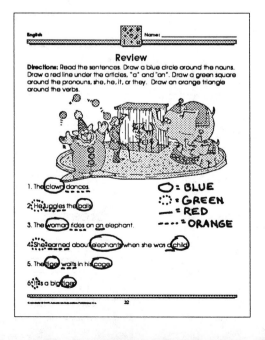

1. The clown dances.

2. He juggles the balls.

3. The woman rides on an elephant.

4. She learned about elephants when she was a child.

5. The tiger waits in his cage.

6. It's a big tiger.

○ = BLUE
◌ = GREEN
— = RED
---- = ORANGE

32

Adjectives

Adjectives are describing words.

Directions: Circle the describing words in the sentences.

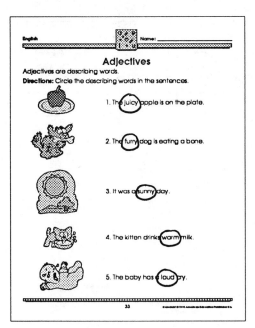

1. The (juicy) apple is on the plate.

2. The (furry) dog is eating a bone.

3. It was a (sunny) day.

4. The kitten drinks (warm) milk.

5. The baby has a (loud) cry.

Statements

Statements are sentences that tell us something. They begin with a capital letter and end with a period.

Directions: Write the sentences on the lines below. Begin each sentence with a capital letter and end it with a period.

1. we like to ride our bikes

We like to ride our bikes.

2. we go down the hill very fast

We go down the hill very fast.

3. we keep our bikes shiny and clean

We keep our bikes shiny and clean.

4. we know how to change the tires

We know how to change the tires.

Adjectives

Directions: Choose a describing word from the word bank to fill in the blanks.

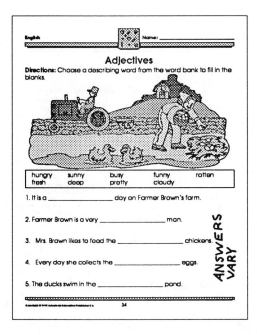

hungry	sunny	busy	funny	rotten
fresh	deep	pretty	cloudy	

1. It is a _____ day on Farmer Brown's farm.

2. Farmer Brown is a very _____ man.

3. Mrs. Brown likes to feed the _____ chickens.

4. Every day she collects the _____ eggs.

5. The ducks swim in the _____ pond.

ANSWERS VARY

Questions

Questions are sentences that ask a question. They begin with a capital letter and end with a question mark.

Directions: Copy the questions on the lines below. Begin each sentence with a capital letter and end it with a question mark.

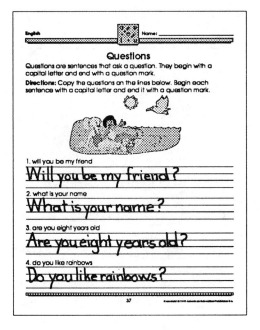

1. will you be my friend

Will you be my friend?

2. what is your name

What is your name?

3. are you eight years old

Are you eight years old?

4. do you like rainbows

Do you like rainbows?

Adjectives

Directions: Think of your own describing words. Write a story about Smokey the cat.

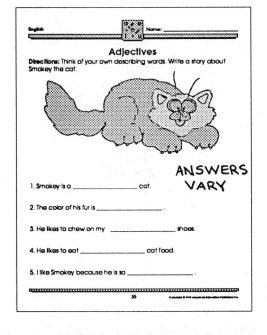

ANSWERS VARY

1. Smokey is a _____ cat.

2. The color of his fur is _____ .

3. He likes to chew on my _____ shoes.

4. He likes to eat _____ cat food.

5. I like Smokey because he is so _____ .

Parts Of A Sentence

Directions: Draw a circle around the naming part of the sentence. Draw a line under the action part of the sentence.

Example: (John) drinks juice every morning.

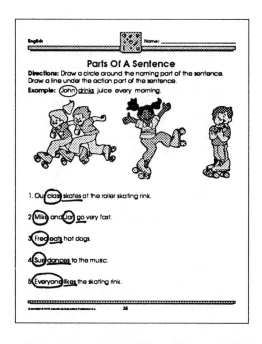

1. Our (class) skates at the roller skating rink.

2. (Mike) and (Jon) go very fast.

3. (Fred) eats hot dogs.

4. (Sue) dances to the music.

5. (Everyone) likes the skating rink.

Parts Of A Sentence

Directions: Look at the pictures. Match a naming part to an action part to make a sentence that tells about the pictures.

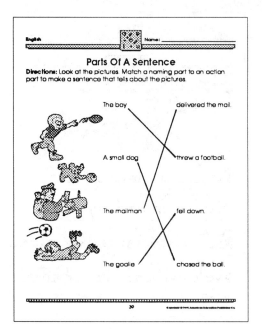

The boy   delivered the mail.

A small dog   threw a football.

The mailman   fell down.

The goalie   chased the ball.

Days of the Week and Months of the Year

The days of the week and the months of the year are always capitalized.

Directions: Circle the words that are written correctly. Write the ones that need capital letters on the lines below.

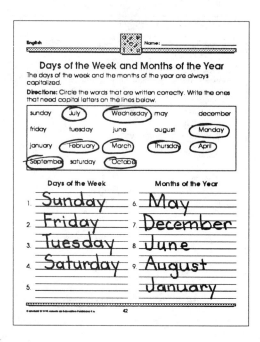

sunday	(July)	(Wednesday)	may	december
friday	tuesday	june	august	(Monday)
january	(February)	(March)	(Thursday)	(April)
(September)	saturday	(October)		

Days of the Week	Months of the Year
1. Sunday	6. May
2. Friday	7. December
3. Tuesday	8. June
4. Saturday	9. August
5.	January

Review

Directions: 1) Write the sentences on the lines below. 2) Begin with a capital letter and end with a period or a question mark. 3) Draw a circle around the naming part of the sentence. 4) Draw a line under the action part of the sentence. 5) Draw a box around the describing words.

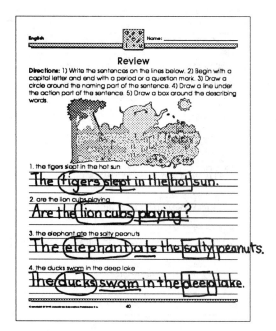

1. the tigers slept in the hot sun

The (tigers) slept in the [hot] sun.

2. are the lion cubs playing

Are the (lion cubs) playing ?

3. the elephant ate the salty peanuts

The (elephant) ate the [salty] peanuts.

4. the ducks swam in the deep lake

The (ducks) swam in the [deep] lake.

Book Titles

The first word and all of the important words in a title begin with a capital letter.

Directions: 1) Write the book titles on the lines below. 2) Use capital letters.

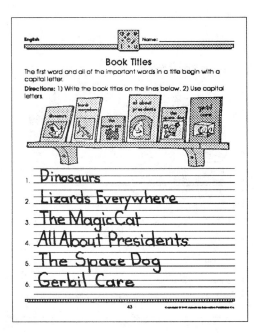

1. Dinosaurs
2. Lizards Everywhere
3. The Magic Cat
4. All About Presidents
5. The Space Dog
6. Gerbil Care

Capitalization: People, Places And Pets

We begin the names of people, places and pets with a capital letter.

Directions: Write the names on the lines below. Use capital letters at the beginning of each word.

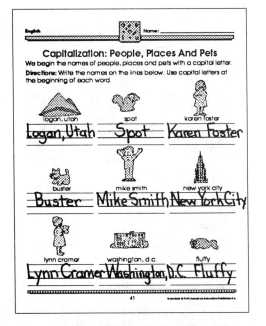

logan, utah   spot   karen foster

Logan, Utah   Spot   Karen Foster

buster   mike smith   new york city

Buster   Mike Smith   New York City

lynn cramer   washington, d.c.   fluffy

Lynn Cramer   Washington, D.C.   Fluffy

Using Is, Are And Am

"Is," "are," and "am" are special action words that tell us something is happening now.
1) We use "am" with "I." Example: I am.
2) We use "is" to tell about one person or thing. Example: He is, it is.
3) We use "are" to tell about more than one. Example: We are.
4) We use "are" with "you". Example: You are.

Directions: Write "is," "are" or "am" in the sentences below.

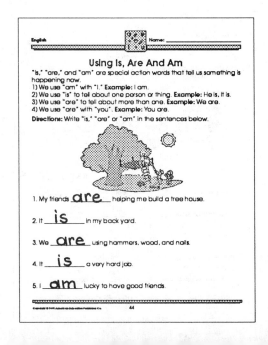

1. My friends **are** helping me build a tree house.

2. It **is** in my back yard.

3. We **are** using hammers, wood, and nails.

4. It **is** a very hard job.

5. I **am** lucky to have good friends.

Using Was And Were

"Was" and "were" tell us about something that already happened.
1) Use "was" to tell about one person or thing. Example: I was, he was.
2) Use "were" to tell about more than one person or thing or when using the word "you". Example: We were, you were.

Directions: Write "was" or "were" in each sentence.

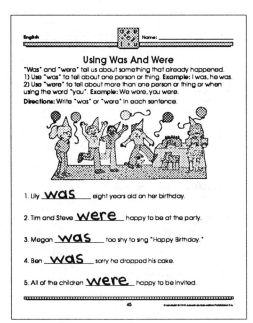

1. Lily **was** eight years old on her birthday.

2. Tim and Steve **were** happy to be at the party.

3. Megan **was** too shy to sing "Happy Birthday."

4. Ben **was** sorry he dropped his cake.

5. All of the children **were** happy to be invited.

45

Review

Directions: Write the sentences, using capital letters for people, places, pets, and book titles.

1. jane and ted are home in athens, ohio.

Jane and Ted are home in Athens, Ohio.

2. amy franks wrote a book called my best friend.

Amy Franks wrote a book called My Best Friend.

3. john's dog is named lucky.

John's dog is named Lucky.

Directions: Write "is," "was," "were," "are" or "am" in the sentences below.

1. We **are** going to school today.
2. Yesterday, we **were** at home.
3. Today, he **is** playing baseball.
4. Yesterday, I **was** sick.

Directions: Write the contractions in the sentences below.

1. **I'm** happy about my baby sister.   I am
2. **She's** a beautiful baby.   She is
3. My parents are happy. **They're** also proud.   They are
4. I gave her a teddy bear. **It's** her favorite toy.   It is

46

Contractions With Is, Am, Are

(A short way to write two words together, such as isn't, I've, and weren't. Example: it is = it's.)

Directions: Draw a line from the words to their matching contractions.

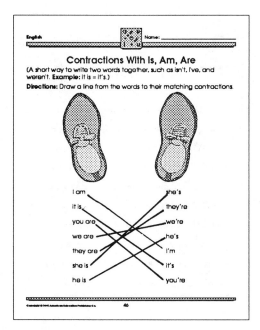

I am   she's
it is   they're
you are   we're
we are   he's
they are   I'm
she is   it's
he is   you're

46

Using Go, Going And Went

We use "go" or "going" to tell about now or later. Sometimes we use "going" with the words "am" or "are." We use "went" to tell about something that already happened.

Directions: Write "go," "going" or "went" in the sentences below.

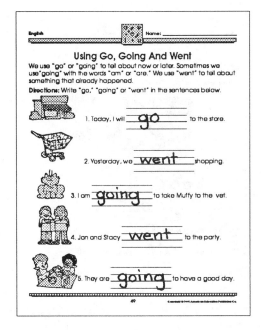

1. Today, I will **go** to the store.

2. Yesterday, we **went** shopping.

3. I am **going** to take Muffy to the vet.

4. Jan and Stacy **went** to the party.

5. They are **going** to have a good day.

49

Contractions With Not

We use contractions with the word not.

Example: do not = don't

Directions: Draw a line from each word pair to its matching contraction.

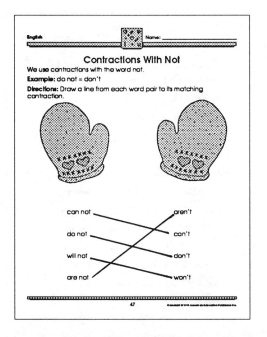

can not   aren't
do not   can't
will not   don't
are not   won't

47

Using Have, Has And Had

We use "have" and "has" to tell about now. We use "had" to tell about something that already happened.

Directions: Write "has," "have" or "had" in the sentences below.

1. We **have** three cats at home.

2. Ginger **has** brown fur.

3. Bucky and Charlie **have** white fur.

4. My friend Tom **had** one cat but he died.

5. Tom **has** a new cat now.

50

Using See, Saw And Sees

We use "see" or "sees" to tell about now. We use "saw" to tell about something that already happened.

Directions: Write "see," "sees" or "saw" in the sentences below.

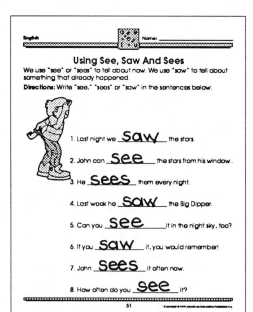

1. Last night we **saw** the stars.

2. John can **see** the stars from his window.

3. He **sees** them every night.

4. Last week he **saw** the Big Dipper.

5. Can you **see** it in the night sky, too?

6. If you **saw** it, you would remember!

7. John **sees** it often now.

8. How often do you **see** it?

Ownership

We add "'s" to nouns (people, places or things) to tell who or what owns something.

Directions: Read the sentences. Fill in the blanks to show ownership. Write the sentences to show ownership.

Example: The doll belongs to Sara.
It is Sara's doll.

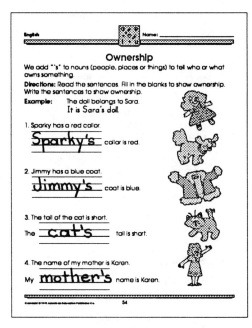

1. Sparky has a red collar.
Sparky's collar is red.

2. Jimmy has a blue coat.
Jimmy's coat is blue.

3. The tail of the cat is short.
The **cat's** tail is short.

4. The name of my mother is Karen.
My **mother's** name is Karen.

Using Eat, Eats And Ate

We use "eat" or "eats" to tell about now. We use "ate" to tell about what already happened.

Directions: Write "eat," "eats" or "ate" in the sentences below.

1. We like to **eat** in the lunchroom.

2. Today, my teacher will **eat** in a different room.

3. At my old school, we **ate** at noon everyday.

4. Yesterday, we **ate** pizza, pears, and peas.

5. Today, we will **eat** turkey and potatoes.

Ownership

Directions: Read the sentences. Choose the correct word and write it in the sentences below.

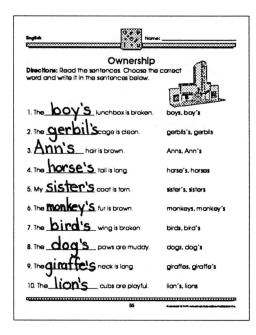

1. The **boy's** lunchbox is broken.　　boys, boy's

2. The **gerbil's** cage is clean.　　gerbils's, gerbils

3. **Ann's** hair is brown.　　Anns, Ann's

4. The **horse's** tail is long.　　horse's, horses

5. My **sister's** coat is torn.　　sister's, sisters

6. The **monkey's** fur is brown.　　monkeys, monkey's

7. The **bird's** wing is broken.　　birds, bird's

8. The **dog's** paws are muddy.　　dogs, dog's

9. The **giraffe's** neck is long.　　giraffes, giraffe's

10. The **lion's** cubs are playful.　　lion's, lions

Using Leave, Leaves And Left

We use "leave" and "leaves" to tell about now. We use "left" to tell about what already happened.

Directions: Write "leave," "leaves," or "left" in the sentences below.

1. Last winter, we **left** seed in the bird feeder everyday.

2. My mother likes to **leave** food out for the squirrels.

3. When it rains, she **leaves** bread for the birds.

4. Yesterday, she **left** popcorn for the birds.

Review

Directions: Choose the correct word to fill in the blanks.

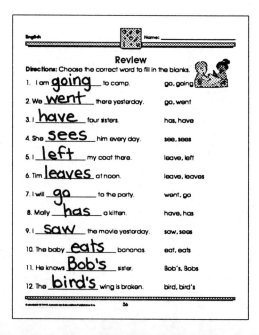

1. I am **going** to camp.　　go, going

2. We **went** there yesterday.　　go, went

3. I **have** four sisters.　　has, have

4. She **sees** him every day.　　see, sees

5. I **left** my coat there.　　leave, left

6. Tim **leaves** at noon.　　leave, leaves

7. I will **go** to the party.　　went, go

8. Molly **has** a kitten.　　have, has

9. I **saw** the movie yesterday.　　saw, sees

10. The baby **eats** bananas.　　eat, eats

11. He knows **Bob's** sister.　　Bob's, Bobs

12. The **bird's** wing is broken.　　bird, bird's

Sentences And Non-Sentences

A sentence tells a complete idea.

Directions: Circle the group of words if it tells a complete idea.

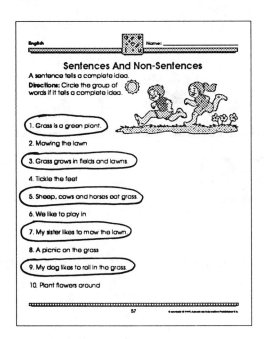

1. (Grass is a green plant.)
2. Mowing the lawn
3. (Grass grows in fields and lawns.)
4. Tickle the feet
5. (Sheep, cows and horses eat grass.)
6. We like to play in
7. (My sister likes to mow the lawn.)
8. A picnic on the grass
9. (My dog likes to roll in the grass.)
10. Plant flowers around

Surprising Sentences

Directions: Put an exclamation point at the end of the sentences that tell a strong feeling. Use a period for sentences that tell something. Use a question mark for sentences that ask a question.

1. We like to dress up like in costumes .
2. We like to surprise Mom .
3. Yikes !
4. Mom always acts surprised .
5. Oh, my !
6. She laughs when we show our faces .
7. She tries to surprise us sometimes .
8. Surprise !
9. We like to pretend we're surprised .
10. Do you like surprises ?

Sentences And Non-Sentences

Directions: Circle the group of words if it tells a complete idea.

1. (A secret is something you know.)
2. (My mom's birthday gift is a secret.)
3. No one else.
4. If you promise not to.
5. (I'll tell you a secret.)
6. Something nobody knows.

Commands

Commands tell someone to do something. **Example:** Be careful. It can also be written as "Be careful!" if it tells a strong feeling.

Directions: 1) Put a period at the end of the command sentences. 2) Use an exclamation point if the sentence tells a strong feeling. 3) Write your own commands on the lines below.

1. Clean your room .
2. Now !
3. Be careful with your goldfish .
4. Watch out !
5. Be a little more careful .

1) answers vary
3) _____
2) _____
4) _____

Surprising Sentences

Tells a strong feeling and ends with an exclamation mark. A surprising sentence may be only one or two words showing fear, surprise or pain. **Example:** Oh, no!

Directions: Put an exclamation point at the end of the sentences that tell a strong feeling. Put a period at the end of the sentences that tell something. Put a question mark at the end of the sentences that ask a question.

1. The cheetah can run very fast .
2. Wow !
3. Look at that cheetah go !
4. Can you run fast ?
5. Oh, my !
6. You're faster than I am .
7. Let's run together .
8. We can run as fast as a cheetah .
9. What fun !
10. Do you think cheetahs get tired ?

Review

Directions: Put a period, an exclamation point or a question mark at the end of the sentences that tell a complete idea. (Remember, commands and surprising sentences can have only one or two words, but can still tell a complete idea.)

1. Jane likes to play ball .
2. Watch out !
3. Sometimes I am afraid I will miss .
4. Pitch the ball to me .
5. Hit it !
6. Run !
7. Faster !
8. Did a great job .

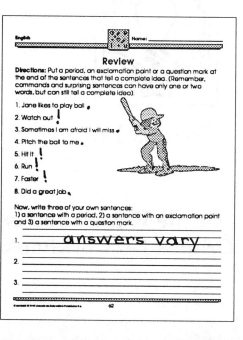

Now, write three of your own sentences:
1) a sentence with a period, 2) a sentence with an exclamation point and 3) a sentence with a question mark.

1. answers vary
2. _____
3. _____

The MASTER SKILLS SERIES

Workbooks for all the basic skills children need to succeed!

Master English

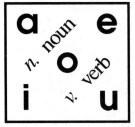

Grades K-6

Master Math

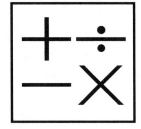

Grades K-6

Master Reading

Grades K-6

Master Comprehension

Grades 1-6

Master Study Skills

Grades 1-6

Master Spelling & Writing

Grades 1-6

Grade K workbooks include 30 lessons plus answer key.
Grades 1-6 workbooks include 62 lessons plus answer key.

NOTES

NOTES

NOTES

END OF ANSWER KEY

Dear Friend:

American Education Publishing is dedicated to designing and developing the highest quality learning materials at the most affordable prices.

The cornerstone of our efforts is a commitment to children and their need for the highest quality education in a competitive world. Our children are the primary asset in America's future. We must provide them with the skills to enrich our proud heritage.

We view the profession of teaching and the responsibility of parenting with the greatest esteem. To ensure that all children experience successful learning requires the involvement and cooperation of home, school, business and the entire community.

It is the objective of American Education Publishing to provide the educational materials and help foster an environment in which students:

✎ Start school and each grade level prepared and ready to learn.

✎ Consistently improve their skill levels in challenging subject matter.

✎ Value and respect the education process and increase their desire for learning.

✎ Gain a level of preparedness for responsible citizenship, further learning and world competition.

Thank you for your dedication to young people.

Name: _____

Verbs

Directions: Write each verb in the correct column.

| rake | talked | look | hopped | skip |
| cooked | fished | call | clean | sewed |

Yesterday

_____

_____

_____

_____

_____

_____

_____

_____

_____

_____

Today

_____

_____

_____

_____

_____

_____

_____

_____

_____

_____

31

Name: _____

Review

Directions: Read the sentences. Draw a blue circle around the nouns. Draw a red line under the articles, "a" and "an". Draw a green square around the pronouns, she, he, it, or they. Draw an orange triangle around the verbs.

1. The clown dances.

2. He juggles the balls.

3. The woman rides on an elephant.

4. She learned about elephants when she was a child.

5. The tiger waits in his cage.

6. It is a big tiger.

Name: _____

Adjectives

Adjectives are describing words.

Directions: Circle the describing words in the sentences.

1. The juicy apple is on the plate.

2. The furry dog is eating a bone.

3. It was a sunny day.

4. The kitten drinks warm milk.

5. The baby has a loud cry.

Name: _____

Adjectives

Directions: Choose a describing word from the word bank to fill in the blanks.

hungry	sunny	busy	funny	rotten
fresh	deep	pretty	cloudy	

1. It is a _____ day on Farmer Brown's farm.

2. Farmer Brown is a very _____ man.

3. Mrs. Brown likes to feed the _____ chickens.

4. Every day she collects the _____ eggs.

5. The ducks swim in the _____ pond.

Name: _____

Adjectives

Directions: Think of your own describing words. Write a story about Smokey the cat.

1. Smokey is a _____ cat.

2. The color of his fur is _____ .

3. He likes to chew on my _____ shoes.

4. He likes to eat _____ cat food.

5. I like Smokey because he is so _____ .

Name: _____

Statements

Statements are sentences that tell us something. They begin with a capital letter and end with a period.

Directions: Write the sentences on the lines below. Begin each sentence with a capital letter and end it with a period.

1. we like to ride our bikes

_____

_____

2. we go down the hill very fast

_____

_____

3. we keep our bikes shiny and clean

_____

_____

4. we know how to change the tires

_____

_____

English Name: _____

Questions

Questions are sentences that ask a question. They begin with a capital letter and end with a question mark.

Directions: Copy the questions on the lines below. Begin each sentence with a capital letter and end it with a question mark.

1. will you be my friend

_____

_____

_____

2. what is your name

_____

_____

_____

3. are you eight years old

_____

_____

_____

4. do you like rainbows

_____

_____

_____

Copyright © 1991 American Education Publishing Co.

Name: _____

Parts Of A Sentence

Directions: Draw a circle around the naming part of the sentence. Draw a line under the action part of the sentence.

Example: (John) <u>drinks</u> juice every morning.

1. Our class skates at the roller skating rink.

2. Mike and Jan go very fast.

3. Fred eats hot dogs.

4. Sue dances to the music.

5. Everyone likes the skating rink.

a e
n. noun
o
v. verb
i u

Name: _____

Parts Of A Sentence

Directions: Look at the pictures. Match a naming part to an action part to make a sentence that tells about the pictures.

The boy   delivered the mail.

A small dog   threw a football.

The mailman   fell down.

The goalie   chased the ball.

Name: _____

Review

Directions: 1) Write the sentences on the lines below. 2) Begin with a capital letter and end with a period or a question mark. 3) Draw a circle around the naming part of the sentence. 4) Draw a line under the action part of the sentence. 5) Draw a box around the describing words.

1. the tigers slept in the hot sun

_____

_____

2. are the lion cubs playing

_____

_____

3. the elephant ate the salty peanuts

_____

_____

4. the ducks swam in the deep lake

_____

_____

Name: _____

Capitalization: People, Places And Pets

We begin the names of people, places and pets with a capital letter.

Directions: Write the names on the lines below. Use capital letters at the beginning of each word.

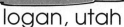
logan, utah
_____
_____

spot
_____
_____

karen foster
_____
_____

buster
_____
_____

mike smith
_____
_____

new york city
_____
_____

lynn cramer
_____
_____

washington, d.c.
_____
_____

fluffy
_____
_____

Days of the Week and Months of the Year

The days of the week and the months of the year are always capitalized.

Directions: Circle the words that are written correctly. Write the ones that need capital letters on the lines below.

sunday	July	Wednesday	may	december
friday	tuesday	june	august	Monday
january	February	March	Thursday	April
September	saturday	October		

Days of the Week

1. _____

2. _____

3. _____

4. _____

Months of the Year

1. _____

2. _____

3. _____

4. _____

5. _____

Name: _____

Book Titles

The first word and all of the important words in a title begin with a capital letter.

Directions: 1) Write the book titles on the lines below. 2) Use capital letters.

1. _____

2. _____

3. _____

4. _____

5. _____

6. _____

Name: _____

Using Is, Are And Am

"Is," "are," and "am" are special action words that tell us something is happening now.

1) We use "am" with "I." **Example:** I am.
2) We use "is" to tell about one person or thing. **Example:** He is, it is.
3) We use "are" to tell about more than one. **Example:** We are.
4) We use "are" with "you". **Example:** You are.

Directions: Write "is," "are" or "am" in the sentences below.

1. My friends _____ helping me build a tree house.

2. It _____ in my back yard.

3. We _____ using hammers, wood, and nails.

4. It _____ a very hard job.

5. I _____ lucky to have good friends.

Name: _____

Using Was And Were

"Was" and "were" tell us about something that already happened.
1) Use "was" to tell about one person or thing. **Example:** I was, he was.
2) Use "were" to tell about more than one person or thing or when using the word "you". **Example:** We were, you were.

Directions: Write "was" or "were" in each sentence.

1. Lily _____ eight years old on her birthday.

2. Tim and Steve _____ happy to be at the party.

3. Megan _____ too shy to sing "Happy Birthday."

4. Ben _____ sorry he dropped his cake.

5. All of the children _____ happy to be invited.

Contractions With Is, Am, Are

(A short way to write two words together, such as isn't, I've, and weren't. **Example:** it is = it's.)

Directions: Draw a line from the words to their matching contractions.

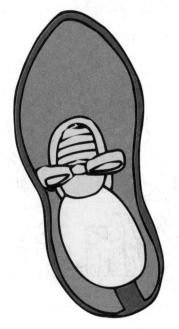 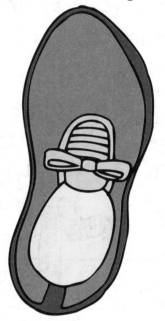

I am	she's
it is	they're
you are	we're
we are	he's
they are	I'm
she is	it's
he is	you're

Name: _____

Contractions With Not

We use contractions with the word not.

Example: do not = don't

Directions: Draw a line from each word pair to its matching contraction.

can not   aren't

do not   can't

will not   don't

are not   won't

47

Name: _____

Review

Directions: Write the sentences, using capital letters for people, places, pets, and book titles.

1. jane and ted are home in athens, ohio.

_____

_____

2. amy franks wrote a book called my best friend.

_____

_____

3. john's dog is named lucky.

_____

_____

Directions: Write "is," "was," "were," "are" or "am" in the sentences below.

1. We _____ going to school today.

2. Yesterday, we _____ at home.

3. Today, he _____ playing baseball.

4. Yesterday, I _____ sick.

Directions: Write the contractions in the sentences below.

1. _____ happy about my baby sister.   I am

2. _____ a beautiful baby.   She is

3. My parents are happy. _____ also proud.   They are

4. I gave her a teddy bear. _____ her favorite toy.   It is

48

Name: _____

Using Go, Going And Went

We use "go" or "going" to tell about now or later. Sometimes we use "going" with the words "am" or "are." We use "went" to tell about something that already happened.

Directions: Write "go," "going" or "went" in the sentences below.

1. Today, I will _____ to the store.

2. Yesterday, we _____ shopping.

3. I am _____ to take Muffy to the vet.

4. Jan and Stacy _____ to the party.

5. They are _____ to have a good day.

Name: _____

Using Have, Has And Had

We use "have" and "has" to tell about now. We use "had" to tell about something that already happened.

Directions: Write "has," "have" or "had" in the sentences below.

1. We _____ three cats at home.

2. Ginger _____ brown fur.

3. Bucky and Charlie _____ white fur.

4. My friend Tom _____ one cat but he died.

5. Tom _____ a new cat now.

Name: _____

Using See, Saw And Sees

We use "see" or "sees" to tell about now. We use "saw" to tell about something that already happened.

Directions: Write "see," "sees" or "saw" in the sentences below.

1. Last night we _____ the stars.

2. John can _____ the stars from his window..

3. He _____ them every night.

4. Last week he _____ the Big Dipper.

5. Can you _____ it in the night sky, too?

6. If you _____ it, you would remember!

7. John _____ it often now.

8. How often do you _____ it?

Name: _____

Using Eat, Eats And Ate

We use "eat" or "eats" to tell about now. We use "ate" to tell about what already happened.

Directions: Write "eat," "eats" or "ate" in the sentences below.

1. We like to _____ in the lunchroom.

2. Today, my teacher will _____ in a different room.

3. At my old school, we _____ at noon everyday.

4. Yesterday, we_____ pizza, pears, and peas.

5. Today, we will _____ turkey and potatoes.

Name: _____

Using Leave, Leaves And Left

We use "leave" and "leaves" to tell about now. We use "left" to tell about what already happened.

Directions: Write "leave," "leaves," or "left" in the sentences below.

1. Last winter, we _____ seed in the bird feeder everyday.

2. My mother likes to _____ food out for the squirrels.

3. When it rains, she _____ bread for the birds.

4. Yesterday, she _____ popcorn for the birds.

Name: _____

Ownership

We add "'s" to nouns (people, places or things) to tell who or what owns something.

Directions: Read the sentences. Fill in the blanks to show ownership. Write the sentences to show ownership.

Example: The doll belongs to Sara.
It is Sara's doll.

1. Sparky has a red collor.

_____

_____ collar is red.

_____

2. Jimmy has a blue coat.

_____

_____ coat is blue.

_____

3. The tail of the cat is short.

_____

The _____ tail is short.

_____

4. The name of my mother is Karen.

_____

My _____ name is Karen.

_____

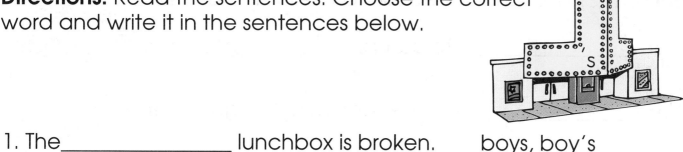

Name: _____

Ownership

Directions: Read the sentences. Choose the correct word and write it in the sentences below.

1. The _____ lunchbox is broken. boys, boy's

2. The _____ cage is clean. gerbils's, gerbils

3. _____ hair is brown. Anns, Ann's

4. The _____ tail is long. horse's, horses

5. My _____ coat is torn. sister's, sisters

6. The _____ fur is brown. monkeys, monkey's

7. The _____ wing is broken. birds, bird's

8. The _____ paws are muddy. dogs, dog's

9. The _____ neck is long. giraffes, giraffe's

10. The _____ cubs are playful. lion's, lions

Name: _____

Review

Directions: Choose the correct word to fill in the blanks.

1. I am _____ to camp.   go, going

2. We _____ there yesterday.   go, went

3. I _____ four sisters.   has, have

4. She _____ him every day.   see, sees

5. I _____ my coat there.   leave, left

6. Tim _____ at noon.   leave, leaves

7. I will _____ to the party.   went, go

8. Molly _____ a kitten.   have, has

9. I _____ the movie yesterday.   saw, sees

10. The baby _____ bananas.   eat, eats

11. He knows _____ sister.   Bob's, Bobs

12. The _____ wing is broken.   bird, bird's

Name: _____

Sentences And Non-Sentences

A sentence tells a complete idea.

Directions: Circle the group of words if it tells a complete idea.

1. Grass is a green plant.

2. Mowing the lawn

3. Grass grows in fields and lawns.

4. Tickle the feet

5. Sheep, cows and horses eat grass.

6. We like to play in

7. My sister likes to mow the lawn.

8. A picnic on the grass

9. My dog likes to roll in the grass.

10. Plant flowers around

n. noun
v. verb
a e
o
i u

Name: _____

Sentences And Non-Sentences

Directions: Circle the group of words if it tells a complete idea.

1. A secret is something you know.

2. My mom's birthday gift is a secret.

3. No one else.

4. If you promise not to.

5. I'll tell you a secret.

6. Something nobody knows.

Name: _____

Surprising Sentences

Tells a strong feeling and ends with an exclamation mark. A surprising sentence may be only one or two words showing fear, surprise or pain. **Example:** Oh, no!

Directions: Put an exclamation point at the end of the sentences that tell a strong feeling. Put a period at the end of the sentences that tell something. Put a question mark at the end of the sentences that ask a question.

1. The cheetah can run very fast

2. Wow

3. Look at that cheetah go

4. Can you run fast

5. Oh, my

6. You're faster than I am

7. Let's run together

8. We can run as fast as a cheetah

9. What fun

10. Do you think cheetahs get tired

Name: _____

Surprising Sentences

Directions: Put an exclamation point at the end of the sentences that tell a strong feeling. Use a period for sentences that tell something. Use a question mark for sentences that ask a question.

1. We like to dress up like in costumes

2. We like to surprise Mom

3. Yikes

4. Mom always acts surprised

5. Oh, my

6. She laughs when we show our faces

7. She tries to surprise us sometimes

8. Surprise

9. We like to pretend we're surprised

10. Do you like surprises

Name: _____

Review

Directions: Put a period, an exclamation point or a question mark at the end of the sentences that tell a complete idea. (Remember, commands and surprising sentences can have only one or two words, but can still tell a complete idea).

1. Jane likes to play ball

2. Watch out

3. Sometimes I am afraid I will miss

4. Pitch the ball to me

5. Hit it

6. Run

7. Faster

8. Did a great job

Now, write three of your own sentences:
1) a sentence with a period, 2) a sentence with an exclamation point and 3) a sentence with a question mark.

1. _____

_____

2. _____

_____

3. _____

_____